About the Author

Interior designer, artist and poet Mahuroos Shafeeq was born in Maldives. In his early teens in Malaysia, he gained his profound interest in poetry as he was introduced to English literature. He learnt, then, the beauty of expressing love and life's myriad emotions. His first unreleased book was based on a project he worked on during his degree at Northumbria University, that won best concept. Since then, he never gave up the idea of releasing his first collection of poetry and becoming a social advocate for individuals who deserve the rights in the community.

Veil of Sorrow

Mahuroos Shafeeq

Veil of Sorrows

Olympia Publishers
London

www.olympiapublishers.com
OLYMPIA PAPERBACK EDITION

A CIP catalogue record for this title is
available from the British Library.

ISBN: 978-1-80439-274-4

This is a work of fiction.
Names, characters, places and incidents originate from the writer's imagination.
Any resemblance to actual persons, living or dead, is purely coincidental.

First Published in 2023

Olympia Publishers
Tallis House
2 Tallis Street
London
EC4Y 0AB

Printed in Great Britain

Dedication

My voice is a dedication to society and its people. It opens a door, welcomes you, encourages you to speak your story, and gives the freedom, your life and soul deserves. Lastly, I dedicate to the little me, you did it!

Acknowledgements

Thank you to my loving family and friends that held my hand through the storms, without them I wouldn't have found the diamond within me, and received the courage to keep writing. Thank you to my lover, who has loved every doubt I had, on becoming who, I dreamt of being. Thank you to the amazing publishing team of Olympia Publishers, for believing in my work and accepting it with such an open mind.

Surrender

I tried to leave you,
when the red flags rose,
but you got me crippled with my past mistakes.
So, I wave my white flag,
to breathe another day.

Blind

I should have known, you were trouble,
when you came buzzed,
took care of you,
when you proved enabled,
forgot to question you,
my bad,
when you've got a history of dilly-dallying your lovers over.
Kept wishing you were high,
the nights you visited me,
so, that you'll see me in a similar light.
But there's no convincing you my worth,
when you're so visually impaired.

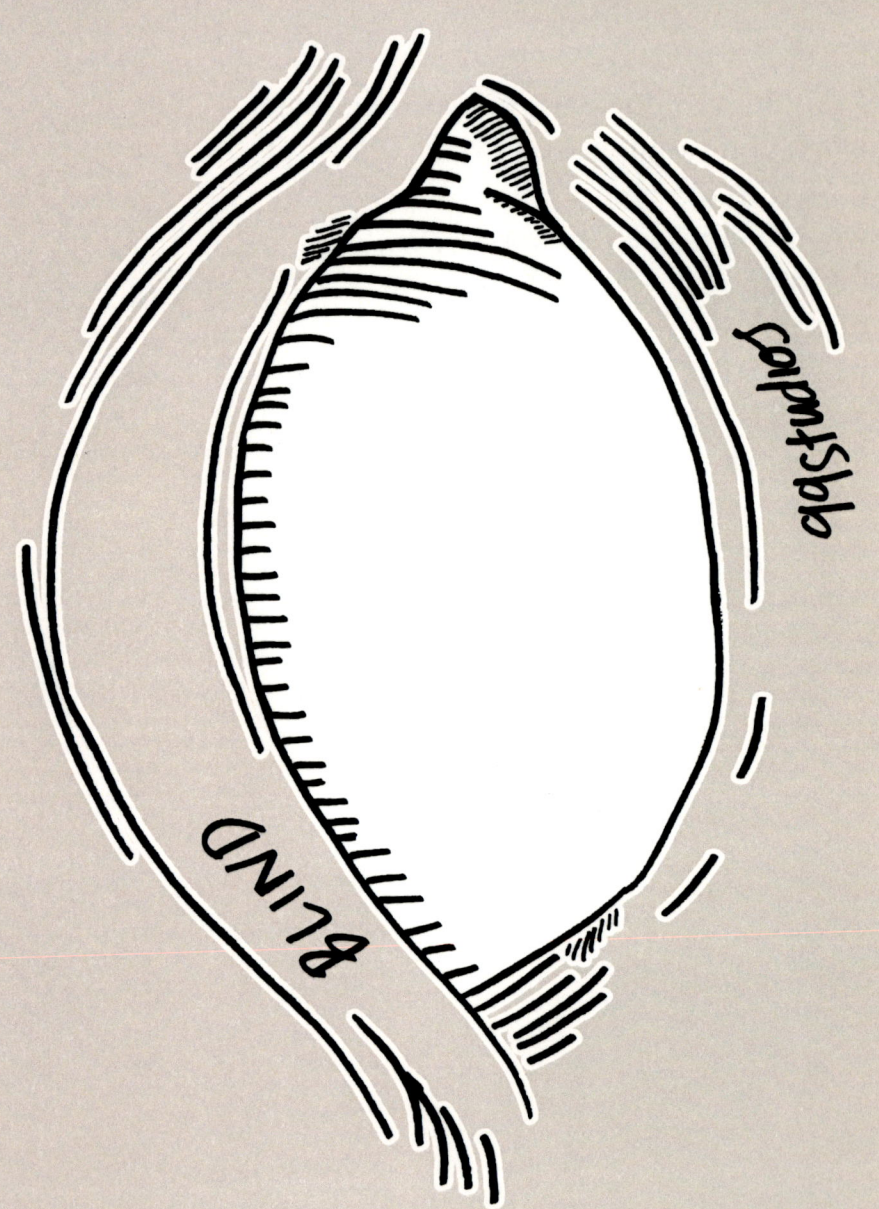

Rebirth

I bathed myself in holy water,
confessed my sins to the holy power,
walls closed,
obtained from mirrors.
Drained my tears into a jar with your label,
carved my wrists with your initials,
exorcised for you to leave my body,
and begged the lord for my purity.

REBIRTH

I'll DO ANYTHING TO FORGET YOU!

99studios

Wingless

Ripped off my wings,
laid them beneath your feet.
Just so, you could fly once again,
never thought you'd fly,
over back to him.

Worthless

I heard you moved on,
knew you get easily manipulated.
So, no shock in knowing you chose the leftovers,
said, you were over him,
yes, a fool.
I believed you,
but I guess your definition of moved on,
was going down on him,
in the wake of laying the same night like me.

The Fool

You should have realized you had everything chivalrous,
the only reason I gave you whole,
but that was never going to be enough.
So, I called it quits,
said I had enough.
I'm not that person,
to live feeling worthless.
You always had your eyes wide for a quick escape,
seeking the worst in me.
Well, you should've mentioned, you liked it that way,
so, I could've kinked you up with my batshit attitude.
Don't you know?
I'm the best you'll ever meet.

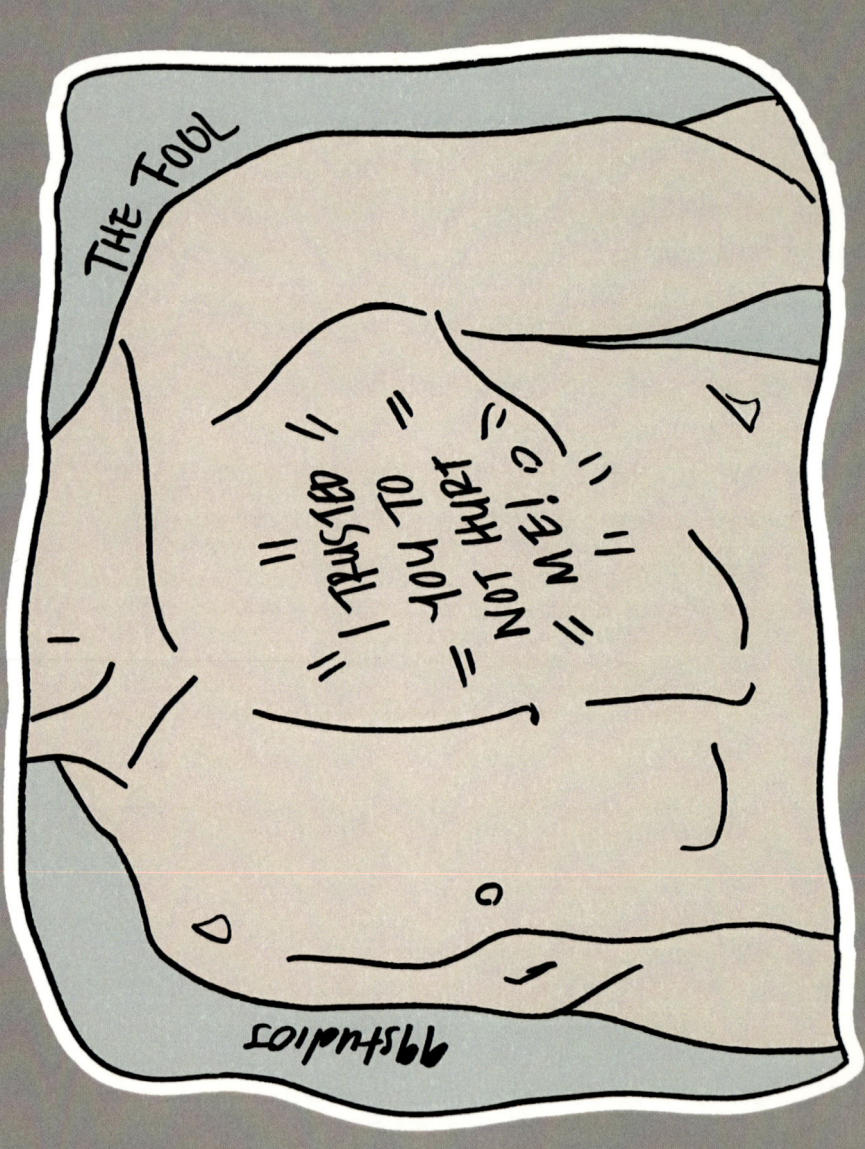

Sorry

Forgive me,
I left you before it got too real.
Maybe I liked you better,
when you felt surreal,

or maybe I just feared,
that you'll leave me,
before I left.

So, I don't know why,
you're still chasing.
When I don't know what to give,
for you and I to begin,
what we just finished.

But it was never your fault,
maybe, I'm just way hard to please.
But I promise you,
you'll find someone to replace me,

And I know you gave it your all,
heck, I know I gave it too,
but it is what it is,
that we were never meant to be.

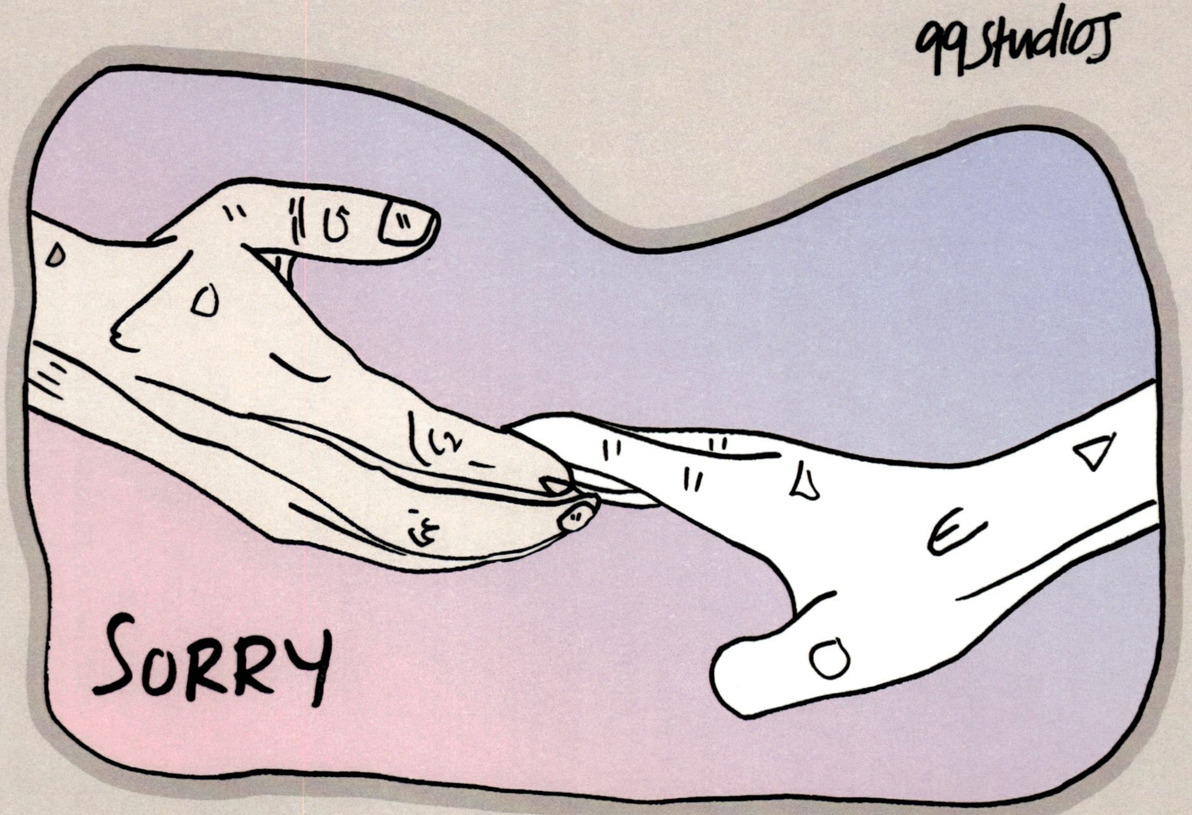
99studios
SORRY

Apparition

It's Friday night,
I'm back home to my desolate headspace,
Foolishly.
I stayed hopeful for your words once again,
supposing you'll be back,
for one final night.
Just so, I get the courage to go our separate ways,
as the memories of our youth,
lingers in my bedroom.
Gave you another attempt,
but received another excuse.
Now, I sway alone in the diminished lights,
to feel the apparition of you again.

Best thing you never had

When we met each other years after our separation, I saw how much you have grown since our teenage romance.

You asked me whether I missed you, wanted you, craved you, and it was neither. My heart did not beat for you any longer, my skin did not feel the bumps, and my mind did not view you as a potential option.

When you kissed me, I did not feel a sense of sorrow your kiss once left on them. That night you said that you regret not seeing the greatness in me, when you had me.

You were right, I became the best version of myself ever since you became the best thing I never had.

Hummingbird

You sang so beautifully that night,
when I came to see you while you were unwell,
I still have that memory of you treasured,
It is the only memory I have kept unerased of ours.
I used to only try searching for hummingbirds after you,
because you showed me how beautiful a human hearts
melody can be.

Cotton Candy Days

Cotton candies filled the setting sky,
as you held me in your arms.
While you told me about your past mistakes,
held you close,
to make you feel safe,
through the storms,
you built in yourself,
always had a habit of keeping safe,
The troubled women who came to take,
ended up giving another piece of myself,
so that you'll find peace again.

The Search

My mama consistently guided me to continue searching
the waters,
said, there were plenty of fish in the ocean,
that, along with the search,
I'll be able to find somebody.
However, she never thought to address,
for what extent I'll be searching,
or how immense the ocean is.

Lovesick

Come back into the sheets,
lay skin to skin,
and love me wild,
because baby,
I'm lovesick for you.

Don't make me beg,
standing there staring at me across the room,
because distance worsens my disease,
so, come back into the sheets,
because it takes two to keep this heart pulsing.

I could feel the danger of loving you this deeply,
but I know you've been in the dark as well,
so, come back,
so, we can nurse this pain,
close the distance between us,
be lovesick together.

Walls Closed

I grabbed you with my palms,
placed gentle kisses onto your sleeping face,
desperately needing your attention,
as we only had expiring time on our hands,
of hiding behind closed walls,
nothing but you and I,
until the sun rose,
awakening the city,
making us once again,
just a Friday night secret.

Attachment

I still got your string,
wrapped around my fingers,
knew that I came out needy,
but I never begged for your loving.

I guess you were right,
I am needy,
but don't think I would be,
if you gave me what I needed.

Forgive me that I came out sensitive,
though, I swear,
I've usually got a hold of my emotions,
but these tears are rolling,
because maybe, I care too excessively.

Knew I shouldn't have leaped,
when you were on the deck still second-guessing.

But you shouldn't have knotted your string firmly,
if you didn't want me to be hanging.

Farewell Kiss

I still recall our last day together,
in the back of the cab, back to your cheap Airbnb.
You asked me whether I would like to go,
drop you off at the transport terminal or return home.
I always was the one to flee from my feelings,
but I was so used to getting hurt anyway,
that I decided to go with a doubtful, yes.

After twenty-five minutes,
you came back with your backpack,
we rode in silence the entire way.
However, the silence never prevented you from trying to
get back my attention,
as you delicately kept nudging my legs for closure.

We spent a while, searching for your vehicle number.
almost giving up.
We eventually managed to catch it,
just before it nearly left without you.

Before you strolled inside,
you caught the woe in your eyes,
and firmly embraced me,
furtively planting on the back of my neck,
with your famous farewell kiss.

The Wanderer

I always knew deep down,
that our time together was brief.
You were way elder than me,
way ahead of my time,
so out of my reach.
You were venturing the world,
seeking different cultures,
tasting various flavors,
in each city,
you laid your feet.

I was a piece of another chapter in your on-going novel,
while you remained in mine,
as a gleaming hope,
of rediscovering what I had felt with you,
back in the summer 2016.

Optimistic

I was young,
I was naïve,
I chased after hearts,
that was intentionally out taking pride,
in breaking optimistic hearts like mine.

Excessiveness

A deeper conversation with your partner will solve and save many conflicts from occurring in the future because every soul requires to be listened to and understood for their silenced words, caused by the disheartened silencer of their past. We often project behaviors that we self-learn and experience in life, especially that are traumatic.
But it is never too late to relearn and change the cycle for a better you and to form a healthier relationship.

Traces

Your past lovers are the traces of how you learned to grow and rediscover yourself.

Player

I know you see me speaking to you,
see me hurt beside you,
but why don't you respond to my emotions,
when you can react to them digitally.

I could feel you holding back,
ghosting me,
saying, you were occupied,
when you prioritize others.

I know you'll never see your faults in this,
when it's this generation's playbook,
to avoid the baggage called attachments.

I know I can't argue with you,
you're not the first to keep ghosting,
afraid to speak up your mind.
In case you'll bring me down,
but know, I'm already cursed,
in being raised into a loveless generation,
with a heart of overflowing affection to give.

Done

"Now, I have seen your true colors."
"Yes, and I'm all the shades of red."

Done

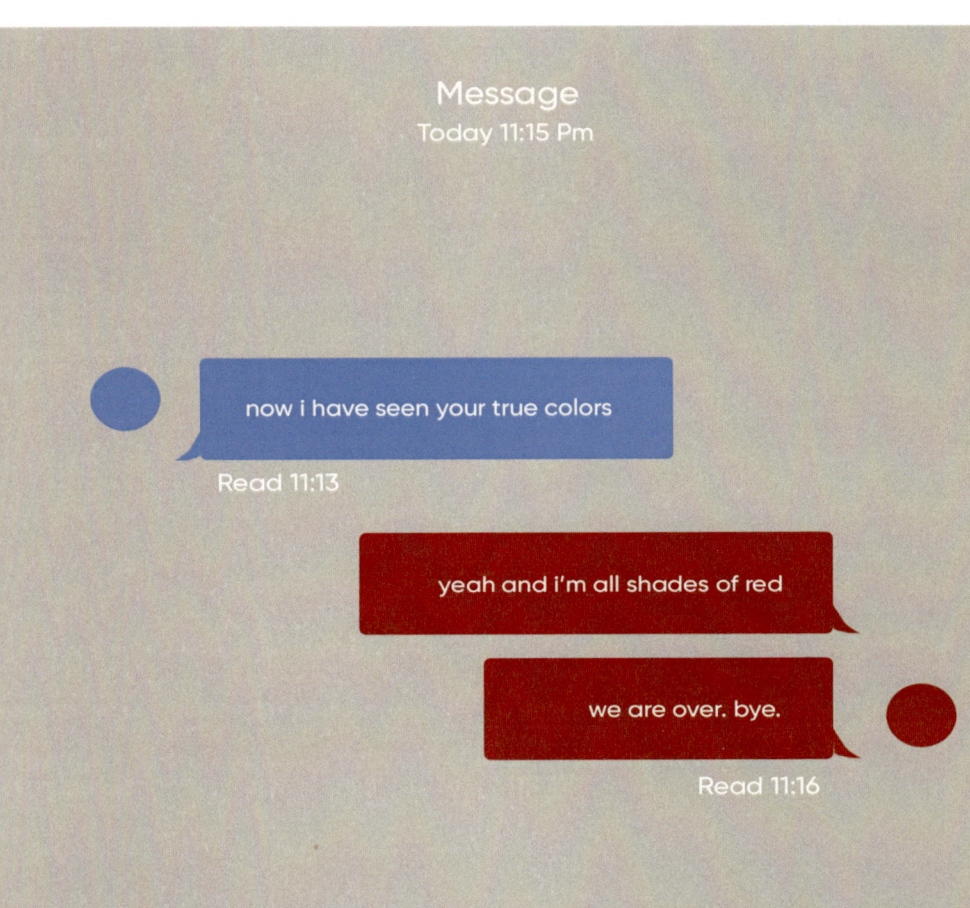

now i have seen your true colors

Read 11:13

yeah and i'm all shades of red

we are over. bye.

Read 11:16

You can't reply to this conversation. <u>Learn More</u>

Checkmate

You can go around making me the bad guy,
because it's orgasmic how you talk lies about me to
our friends,
so, keep talking about me,
keep making yourself the victim.
I love seeing you threatened,
by who I'm becoming.
Guess, I'm no longer the weaker one,
now that I'm in control of your game,
playing it smarter than you ever played me.

CHECKMATE

Calling Out

Do you think you look so cool?
Bringing me down in front of your friends.
trying to look so smart,
threatening me with abandonment,
for not giving you enough time.
I apologize for being too busy making a name of myself,
perspiring blood for our future,
when all you do, is come unappreciative and
empty-handed.

One Sided

Stop tiptoeing down the sidelines,
before I turn you into one of my sides.
You know where I'm coming from.
Now you've got me bored.
Swiping for a better connection,
should've gone with my intuition,
before I chose you and made her the side.
Girl, don't you know you're just wasting time,
tiptoeing down the sidelines,
when I could've been getting better,
rather than receiving this half-hearted love.

Why?

Sometimes we invalidate ourselves to the nature of
someone's behavior.
Before pausing for a brief moment and asking a
simple why?

Our human nature is built that way,
where our anger disrupts all systems of our heart,
by lighting a fuse to our mind.

By taking action to hurt the other person the same,
but worse than how they hurt us.
As if that's our way to victory.

But the real victory is not by getting even,
or neither winning.
It is by carefully rewiring and conjoining your heart
and mind,
to compromise to understand the situation from a
broader perspective.

Warmth

No, I didn't want to interfere,
but I couldn't help but notice,
the way you were watching me on the dance floor,
while kissing him, as I kissed mine.

I know I should probably keep my mind off things
that aren't' mine,
but my mind can't help but replay and wonder,
how those lips could've tasted on mine last night.

So, why don't you stop lying?
And come test these waters,
I swear,
I'll have it warm for you,
just the way you like it.

Never Again

You always had a fetish for the way I moan,
when you gripped my neck for pleasure.
But day after day,
your grip around my neck became rougher and tighter,
that it became a routine of yours that I had no control over.
You often apologized right after,
but I never learned to sympathize,
for the way you made me beg for breath,
to stroke your ego,
and hurt me once again.

Together

I am I.
You are you.
Brought together by an epiphany of curiosity.
Woefully smitten by the loneliness that inhabited each other's hearts.
So fearful of the darkness, we experienced by the isolation from our loved ones,
that we carried each other through the tides until we found ashore,
and called it our new home.

Bloom

Call me by my familiar name,
just like the last time you did.
As you chased me down the meadow of lilies,
I lose all my senses to your loving gaze.
Now that I'm nothing but your name.
But the season has long passed.
So, will you still love me in the season lilies wilt,
just like you did in the season of their bloom?

Perfume

You always referred to me as your perfume,
so, I kept spraying little by little of myself onto you.
Keeping you latched to my scent,
even though I knew it would be over soon,
I stayed selfish to my desires.
For the feeling of being loved for something about myself,
that I never knew was valuable.
Even though we both knew the bittersweet reality to
our ending,
as one day you would walk out into the world,
replacing me with another.
Once again,
leaving me empty.

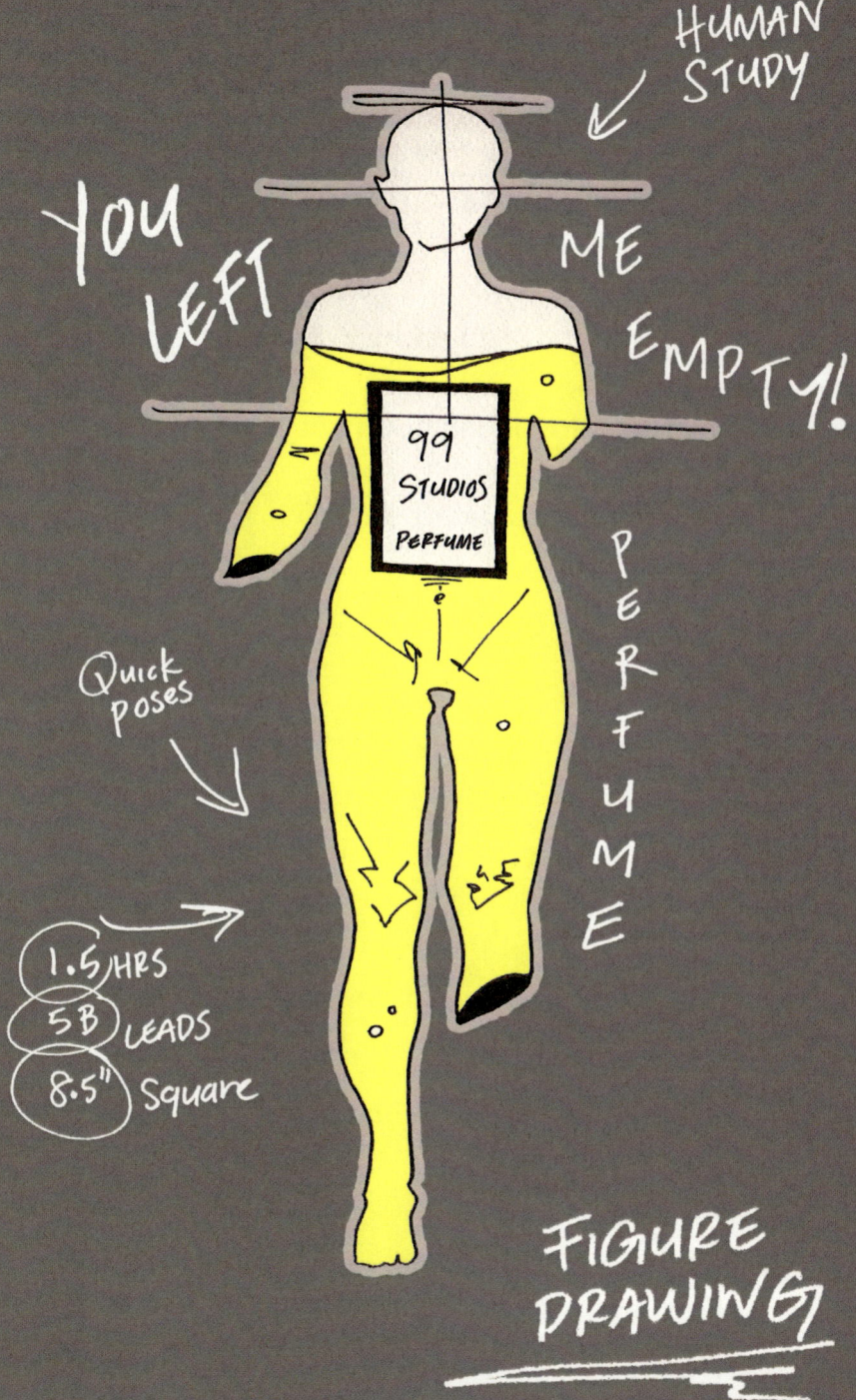

The Wanderer Part Two

Scream your last affections for me,
over the dying sun.
So, it could pass the news of our farewell,
to the awakening moon.

As our first nights apart will endure our most
treasured memories,
to glisten over the cloudless climes and starry skies.

I am finding myself desperately attempting endless ways to
collect constellations,
in the hope of our fates aligning.

With taunting flashbacks of how you selfishly walked away,
wandering on a mission for your own self-discovery.

Climax

Your fingers inside my body, fill me up with an
adrenaline rush,
like rhythmic melodies strumming every muscle and bone
like an electric guitar.

Heroes

We are desperate to create this mirage of ourselves.
To stay relevant that we shed apart every imperfection
gifted to us by molding them to become a duplicate
of another,
who sacrificed by passing us their voice.
So that, we could question the life within our box.

Endeavor

Detachment feels like chasing after lose string kites during springtime.
Sometimes letting go is always disappointing, followed by heavy tears, but we always come back braver to challenge the wind for a second attempt.

We are My Mother's Dreams

My mother gave lives to us by sacrificing her dreams.
Shattering her heart into pieces of four,
and placing them in each of us.

Watching us grow up with her god gifted skills,
conquering the world, that she had always dreamt,
but couldn't due to our struggles in poverty.

Death

"I'm aging," she often says to me.
Without a thought, I replied with, "No, you're not."

Later on,
as I grew older,
I realized that she was slowly preparing us with the thought,
before she honestly said her farewell.

Territory

Don't be afraid to share your story about being taken
advantage of,
it makes you powerful not fragile.

Don't be afraid to expose the people who took your inno-
cence against your will.
Since they never asked for your consent before they
entered your territory.

Courage

Listen,
you have all the right to speak up,
because you don't have to carry their guilt inside
of you.

Listen,
you are not the only one to have this happen to,
or be unable to speak the truth.

So, speak up,
for all humankind,
who have or are going through this barbarity,
just so they could get the courage,
to speak up about their story.

Imagine

There are uncalculatable measures of individuals who
have experienced assault,
but unfortunately, are too afraid to speak up about
the issue,
due to the fear of their family's reputation coming
to shambles,
or due to the dismay of their society not understanding
the seriousness of the issue,
and not taking proper actions.

But imagine how strong we'll be,
If we all came together, united,
and acknowledged the crime,
starting a revolution,
to get justice for their barbaric act,
to reclaim what was once ours.

Mantra

Sometimes you have to remind yourself that all your
problems will wash away,
possibly not right away.
But with the hope of saying it long enough,
you'll start believing it.

Kiss of Karma

If he got caught cheating,
mentally murder him,
Wear the dress he called "too slutty,"
paint your lips crimson,
slide your feet through your highest stilettos,
strut straight into his funeral.
Lay a delightful kiss of karma onto his forehead,
and walk away.

Illusions

I abandoned the thought of labeling every stranger I
met as my possible soulmate.
Began seeing them as just a wandering soul seeking
a purpose,
caged my heart and freed my soul to live in the moment.
Becoming the best version of myself that I grew to know,
with every stranger I knew and grew to adore,
I began living in my youth.
Documenting all the memories of my life,
so, I could play them one day,
when everything had changed,
and time had aged me gracefully,
without regrets,
just nostalgic tears of joy.

Purest of Hearts

Some people come into your life unexpected,
watering your soul with all the nutrition
that requires you to grow into the tall and
magnificent tree,
that you have become today.

But some come with sharpened axes,
to strike you down from how much you have grown,
to see you stumble down to where they stand.
That's when you realize the darkest and the purest
of hearts.

Self-Esteem

You build up my self-esteem like building blocks,
to push them back down again.

Silver Platter

You place the words,
"You're special"
"You're beautiful"
onto a silver platter,
and hand them over to me.
But when I reach out for it,
you let it go,
shattering it to millions.

Helpless

Under the covers,
I found shelter,
until you made it unsafe again.

You grabbed me by my ankles,
dragging me to the edge of the bed,
sewing my lips with a deadly threat.

Then you tore my clothes,
clawed my body,
crawled inside me,
and devoured my childhood,
to fill up your manhood.

HELPLESS

Real Monsters

Some children at the age of seven feared monsters that hid underneath their beds or closets.
Whereas, I feared the monster that roamed around my adolescence with the mask of my relative.

Psycho

Not all predators prey at dawn.
Most hide in plain daylight,
preying on innocent cubs,
playing alone in playing alone together,
away from their mothers' sight.
In the end,
leaving them hollow,
in search of their missing limb.

Mother Earth

With different mixes of soil,
mother earth birthed me into her world,
with the ability to provide life,
to withering blooms,
wherever I laid my feet.

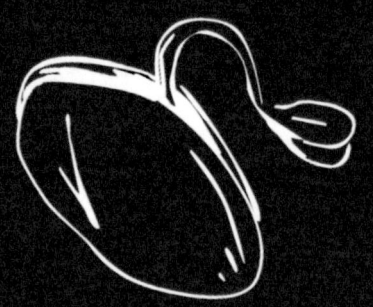

Power

They say we pick our own poison, and I have decided
to drink it myself, rather than let you pour it down
my throat.
At least that way I have dominance over myself when
you decide to destroy what we have.

Body Talk

Leave your feelings by the entryway,
come in, and let's get physical.
and find a solution to our situation.
We'll do it throughout the night,
until we make sense of what we're aching for.

Faded Love

We found faded love,
but I'm still hanging on,
thinking you'll change,
thinking I'll change,
from our criminal behavior.

Weaker Guy

The day you betrayed my trust, you begged me for another chance and to stay despite the fact that you were not the one who would be visually seeing him with you every living, breathing, day and night. You know I always loved you, despite the arguments, and toxicity, but something about this, has no way of erasing them. With utmost honesty, I do not feel strong enough to fight my anxiety against it, and to second guess when the second knife would pierce through my heart again.

Screw Up

Infidelity is a choice; we never unknowingly cheat on
our partner.
It is a choice to be faithful and not give in to the temptations
of the world.
And if we do, we always either get rewarded for our loyalty
or pay the consequences for our disloyalty.

Warrior

Father,
you have carried all the weight of the world,
on your shoulders for so many years,
without grumbling.
You return home,
weightless like a quill,
heavenly rays illuminating you,
passion and love overflowing you,
even though you were ready to collapse.
You still carried yourself through the storms,
head above clouds,
halo levitating over your head,
a grin on your overtired face,
to shroud your scars and blood you bled,
throughout the wars,
you battled.
Just so, we never had to.

One Day

Father,
you are the reason,
I'll never let my child be apprehensive.
To pick up a doll instead of a toy car,
you saw me more than what I could've been.
With no judgment,
you allowed me to make my own decisions.
You chose my interests,
over the society's norm.
Now,
I stand tall,
with all that you educated me,
glad of whom I've become.
Proud to pass all the wisdom I gained from you,
to my very own,
one day.

Pride and Honor

When I look at my reflection,
I see my father gazing back at me,
in all his youth and glory.
Making me slightly smirk,
while fixing his favorite tie around my neck.
Making myself prepared,
to step out and carry his name,
with pride and honor.

After You

This is how I spent my days after you. I wake up every morning glowing, thankful for another chance to do better. I saw the true meaning of love through my own eyes and no longer from yours, it made me bloom.
To shine the diamond in the rough and that helped me to brighten my life and everything in it.

I learned the only way, to clear the dark skies, is to provide light in it.
Without my own efforts, change was inevitable.

I noticed there were others just like me,
attempting to mend themselves, and I selflessly became more empathetic towards people, it showed me the extent of my care.
And I learned to acknowledge it as my greatest gift.

I rediscovered the comfort of my bed, to identify it as a sanctuary of solitude, rather than a place of grief.
Through the pain you put me through, forgiving myself was the most difficult
act of kindness, I had ever given myself.

It took me immense courage and strength to arrive back into life, but something worthwhile, because I regained my purpose and the beauty of existing in it,
with or without you in it.

Thanks!

You never thought your cruel intentions would turn into my best work of poetry.
I promise, I never chose revenge upon you. To haunt your life, whenever your friends tossed my name around you with praises but you should have known, better not to kiss and leave a writer in the dark.

Morning Routine

Every morning,
I put on a valiant face,
gaze at my reflection in the mirror,
and play around with it,
like a piece of dough,
stretching it out,
tucking some in,
as if it's going to change,
the form of my appearance.

Stop the War!

Missiles drop on our homeland, like downpour once used to gush down our narrow and familiar lanes, with puddles to hop in with our friends yet. Now it's flooded with blood and tears of those, who we once used to play with consistently. Our days, now, are mostly spent numbered, hiding away in shelters with an expiry date written upon our fates. So dreadful of death, yet with an increasing measure of hope for a superior tomorrow.

Euphoria

Do you ever notice the scars caused by others, healing and just smile out of euphoria?
It's somehow, liberating to see their overwhelmingly lethal powers, gradually fading over you.

Dignity

I wish I could wreck you the same manner you did to me,
once upon a time.
But that would be degrading myself to become a clone
of you.
And that's someone I don't aim towards becoming, no
matter how low I may be feeling.

Reality

The bitter truth is,
we hear what we want to hear,
we feel what we want to feel,
no matter how much someone,
tries to apologize and clarify,
themselves to us.

Shame

I understand, that you are going through the shame that society had put on you, over the assault that you never merited. I know, it might be difficult to see through the thickness of the haze, but I hope it dissipates, simply even a little, to gradually find your way out of it because there's so much light waiting for you beyond that border of haziness.

Second Chance

Exhale all your restraint feelings for me,
lay all your doubts over my palms,
as I untangle them for you,
so, that we can restart like new,
from the very beginning.

Adulthood

Your own,
flesh and blood,
released you.
Into the abyss,
drowning you,
into its,
unknown pit,
like anchors,
shackled around,
your ankles.
The ghostly tide,
weighting upon you,
pulling you,
into the very depths,
of your fears.

Undesirable

Picked up a dagger,
from the piece of mine that you shattered,
the only piece of mine that had mattered,
into the piece I stared,
As my identity slowly faded,
the more I lacerated into my flesh of flaws,
that you decided weren't desirable enough, anymore.

Someone New

I've searched,
amongst a dozen crowded faces,
pushed and shoved me,
through a dozen bodies,
to find the same warmth,
you ignited within me.
While you thoughtlessly,
lent them to someone new.

Poison Apple

Your venomous words,
slithered out your tongue,
and has built a home,
in the back of my mind,
leaving me contaminated.

Hypocrite

You protest for growth,
but fear of me changing.

Sinners

Truth be told,
we are all sinners,
judging and sinning differently.

Unappreciative

You had heaven granted to you,
between her thighs,
but you never merited.
Instead urged for more,
than she could've offered.
Now you're locked out of heaven,
stuck with just a torturous illusion,
vengeful to reclaim the once reality,
of the one that slipped under your grip.

You're Out Looking for Sugar

How many jars of honey have you dipped your fingers in,
before you came thirsty for mine?

Oh! A Thought!

Have you ever thought of me, the same way you thought of all your past lovers, while you were mine?

Friends or Foe

Funny how we're now friends,
even though we were foes,
distance apart did us swell,
even though we said farewell,
now it's been almost a year,
since the time I watched you disappear.
Look how we've now sprouted,
from the time we doubted,
our ability to find a middle ground,
since the time we almost cut throats,
in the conflicted battlefield we started.

Reminder

The biggest mistake I've made with you, was that we screwed. When I should've respected myself enough to say, "make love to me." But I feared the tone of desperation, which might've followed along with it to have driven you away.

Desperate

You could've spat on me,
dangled me over a cliff,
held my head underwater,
and I would've still cried for more.

Growth

I'm grateful for the way you hollowed out my heart,
If not, I wouldn't had been able to grow seeds out in them,
creating a trail, that I could look back and appreciate
how far
I've come.

Love Yourself

Would you fall in love with yourself in the eyes of the man, that had decided otherwise?

eyes
neve
li

ybe
will
day
ne

Stop!

Quit dwelling in the past.
Attempting to resurrect dead connections,
when not, everything inanimate deserves to be brought
back into your life.

Pinata Heart

Why do you keep letting people, swarm around your piñata heart
oppress it over and over again, and then expect candies to drop out of them?

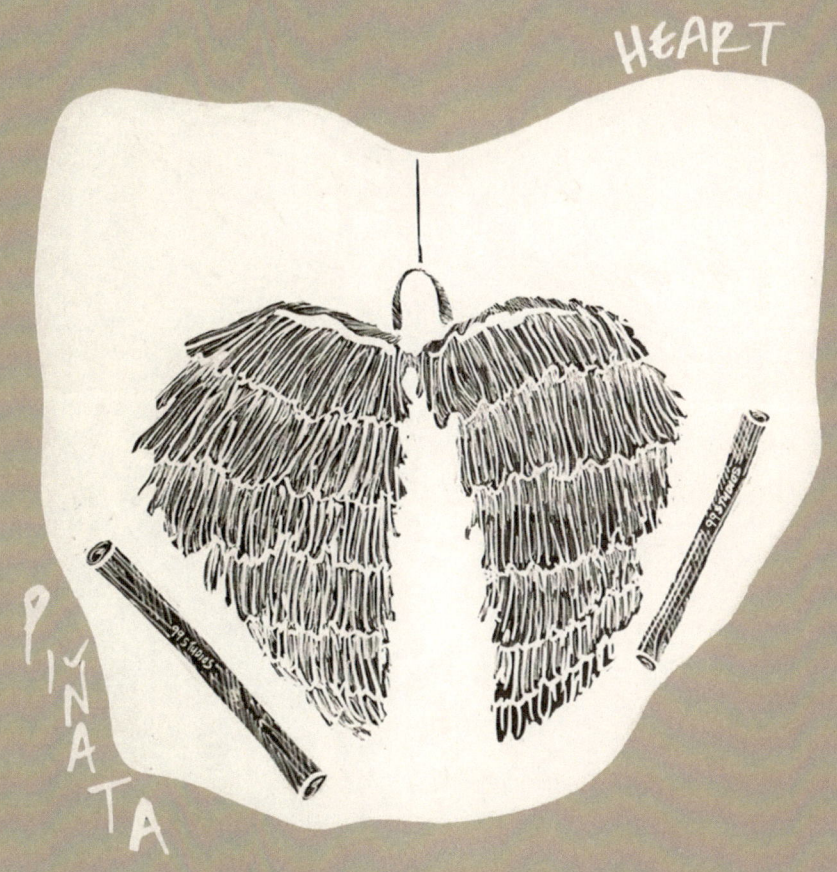

HEART

PIÑATA

Validation

You'll start to realize things about yourself that's lacking.
When you begin to invade the other persons' mind,
in order to find validation of your own worth,
even though they are completely silent.

Haunting

Depression's like an old companion,
no matter how many times,
you overshadow the history,
the memories will always exist,
with haunting belittling voices,
latched deep into your skin,
never truly letting you escape,
the internal horror, of finding eternal sunshine.

Hello, depression

No matter how many companions I try to make,
I always end up arriving to the same old friend,
that had existed with me since the age of fifteen.

Expectations

Everything you touch, turns into lilac.
When you swore, I'll be blossoming in gold.

Oh, so worthy

All I wanted was, for us, to be whimsical lovers.
But I had a habit of creating fantasies in my head,
illusions of the reality, of who they really were,
or what we could've been.
Yet, I still chased after them like a dog that needs water,
convincing myself that late night flings were
enough satisfaction.
When all I should've been convincing myself that I thirsted
for more self-love than pleasure from heartless strangers to
feel whole.

Affair

Fury rages up my veins,
like hard liquor on a winter evening.
Roofied on your lies,
that you dozed me last night,
like you almost planned it overnight.
But I like the way you do it,
trick and treats to heal it.
But if only you could've made me believe it,
maybe then I could've changed it.
Figured out a way,
to stop you from losing grip,
and overdose over my loving.
Battle the cadence of enticement,
in your worn-out jeans that you bought pre-fall.
Then we could have been ride or die,
chasing after trains,
instead of these wrecks.

Victim

At age of innocence,
I witnessed my universe,
ripple open to manhood.
My flesh disintegrated,
the heart became ash,
like pile of dead ember.
Beneath you,
I was a corpse,
left to decompose.
After your temporary trill,
my eyes had been parched for months.
However,
I felt the first drizzle,
pour out and drain me.
Into the ground,
I had been laying helplessly,
between death and seclusion.
But my prayers managed to reach,
miracle of hope grew beneath me,
sprouting roots into my ribcage.
my faith strengthened,
and my purity was restored,
for the crime I did not commit.

Will I Find it?

The nothingness filtered into my room,
thought I had escaped the sorrows,
that had ripened within me with age.
But it has always kept me restless at midnight,
missing the one's I've ever loved.
But you're still lodged into my mind,
no matter how hard I've tried to consume myself to death,
From the memory of you,
us,
but my mind over clouded.
And I try to operate my heart to corporate,
to the thumping of yours,
but it's always beating off rhythm,
So, I attempt to make an instrument,
out of my labyrinthine unexpressed words,
clogged in the back of my throat,
but my dreams had never been my companion.
So, I learned to drown myself in bottles of fantasies,
that I've read in fictional novels,
in possibilities of grasping eternal rapture,
that I've never been able to capture.
By always watering wilted blooms,
in graveyards of strangers,
that I've buried in attempts to root,
a better version of myself,
that I had felt once with you.

How Do I Survive?

Depression is an all-consuming disease.
Some people are born with it,
then there are others who grow into it.
It invades you like the simplest fever,
and as the days pass, it keeps expanding.
Spreading all over your system,
disrupting every cell in you.
We often try to obliterate it
with endless therapies and prescriptions,
but truthfully,
there's no real antidote for it.
You just remain stuck with it,
as if you are spiraling backwards.
And through it, all you begin to reflect back,
to all the good you have and lived through in life.
Then a sudden heavy force of negativity sinks in your chest,
changing all the high into nothingness,
and suddenly the universe goes dark on you.
Eventually,
engulfing you a stray in it.

Act of the Year

People usually say "you're fine",
to refrain from dealing with other people's emotions.
even though the person is mentally suffering
and desperately asking you for strength and guidance
But those negative and thoughtless words you feed them,
live with them overtime.
Misleading them into believing
that they're actually mentally fine,
If they just swept everything under the carpet,
and they begin to wear that hope of a momentary cure,
proud like a necklace for everyone to see and applaud.
But the moment the show is all over,
the curtains are drawn,
the lights dim out,
and the crowds no more.
They turn back to their solitary state,
in the murk undisguised,
embodying the next day persona,
in hopes of achieving the acceptance,
they were beseeching to receive from you.

I Gave it a Shot!

March became her presence again and the night sky gleamed back to glee.

As if the sorrow never existed in this city. But something was unfamiliar around this time.

That the emotions felt almost new. The heat, the warmth felt raw and honest. With every wildest dream I dreamt of crossing over to her world, it felt like she had already beaten me to the ribbon to convince my darkest doubts that there could be a light with one last try. For once I wasn't falling. Every inch I had fallen in the past, it felt like she had fallen an inch deeper in love with me each time we were together. I still wondered how long will I be playing with fire before it burnt me again. But being with her I had learned to be the coziest in places that felt the coldest. Love arrived in the time of my cure, it had me demanded to be felt and embraced but pleading, it must leave now, before I lose all hope of finding it again with someone potentially better.

I Blamed Myself Now What?

It's not the reality I was hurting from anymore.
I was suffering from my imagination of you,
reminiscing on the love I unconditionally gave you.
Now I'm back to the point of despising you.
You had me believed that you've changed,
by the clownery you painted on my face.
Knew you were the one hurting this time around,
gave you a shoulder for your constant mourning,
over your previous heartbreak.
But I never deserved this heartache.
Had me bandaging your self-harm over your drastic ways,
from your street rat days.
So, now I must replace you,
putting back the same pieces you broke,
in order for you to feel superior again.
Never knew how evil you could've proved me,
but congrats,
a round of applause,
because you had now topped yourself number one in
my pages.